Best Wine Buys
At Under-A-Fiver 2001

Ned Halley

foulsham
LONDON • NEW YORK • TORONTO • SYDNEY

foulsham
The Publishing House
Bennetts Close, Cippenham, Berkshire SL1 5AP, England

ISBN 0-572-02643-9

Text copyright © 2001 Ned Halley

Series, format and layout design © 2001 W. Foulsham & Co. Ltd

All rights reserved.

The right of Ned Halley to be identified as the author of this work has been asserted in accordance with the Copyright, Designs and Patents Act 1988.

The Copyright Act prohibits (subject to certain very limited exceptions) the making of copies of any copyright work or of a substantial part of such a work, including the making of copies by photocopying or similar process. Written permission to make a copy or copies must therefore normally be obtained from the publisher in advance. It is advisable also to consult the publisher if in any doubt as to the legality of any copying which is to be undertaken.

Printed in Great Britain by Cox & Wyman Ltd, Reading.

CONTENTS

A personal note	4
The choice	7
The state of the market	9
The price of wine	13
Wine on the web	15
Cross-Channel shopping	17
The best buys	21
The retailers	25
Asda	26
Booths	31
Booze Buster	36
Bottoms Up	36
Co-op	37
First Quench	43
Londis	49
Majestic	52
Oddbins	60
Safeway	65
Sainsbury's	72
Somerfield	84
Tesco	92
Thresher	104
Unwins	104
Victoria Wine	111
Waitrose	111
Wine Cellar	123
Wine Rack	127
A brief vocabulary	128
Wine rituals	151
Wine and food	154
Index	156

A personal note

Welcome to the new edition of what is, in the words of one reviewer of last year's *Best Wine Buys at Under-A-Fiver*, 'the guide to buying the wines most of us actually drink, most of the time'.

It's true. Nine out of every ten bottles of wine bought retail in this country cost less than £5. But wine writers tend to devote nine out of every ten column inches to bottles costing rather more. It's understandable, I suppose.

Compiling my second edition of this book has, however, hardly been an onerous task. There are hundreds of very drinkable wines to be found at under a fiver, and a good many of them represent considerably better value than higher-priced brands.

If anything, the choice under £5 looks set to increase. Downward pressure on prices in a very competitive market, combined with a modest (if wholly unwarranted) 4p rise in duty per bottle in the last budget and sterling's continued strength against most foreign currencies, should mean lower prices all round – or at any rate reasonable stability.

And there's another reason for optimism on the price front. During the recent years of rapid growth in the quality wine market, producers in many regions of the world have been planting new vineyards. Argentina and Chile, Australia and South Africa are expanding production fast – probably too fast. The British trade – a major force in the wine world because this country imports more good wine than any other – is predicting that supply will soon outstrip demand.

So, we can look forward to a continuing torrent of decent wine at sensible prices. But, as always, there's a downside. This is the spectre of the dreaded 'global brand' – wines made on a vast scale, offered at generous discounts to retailers, and supported by expensive advertising campaigns. The problem is that shops find these well-known products a lot easier to sell than unheard-of, but infinitely more interesting, wines from small-scale vineyards.

Pity the supermarket wine buyer. Faced with the choice between stocking up with Blossom Hill or Gallo from a giant UK importer with highly efficient delivery and tempting discounts, and a Portuguese single-vineyard wine from a producer with little English and even less export experience, why do it the hard way? It is very tempting indeed to overlook the obvious fact that the wine from Portugal is much more delicious, and no more expensive, than the big American brands.

Thus do branded wines gradually elbow the little guys off the shelves of the big retailers. It's partly laziness on the part of the supermarkets and chains, but it's more to do with the policies of large companies whose boards have more of an eye on their balance sheets and share prices than they do on the quality and range of products they offer to customers.

At least that's the way I see it. But for the moment, the choice is pretty good, and there's no question that all those discounts – even if only offered on the big brands – do come in handy. Throughout the year, you can expect to find dozens of wines reduced in one way or another, usually by £1 or so a bottle, or on a 'multibuy' basis. You know the sort of thing: buy two, save £2, or buy three and get a fourth bottle free.

In this edition, I have adopted a scoring system to give my entirely subjective opinion of the quality and value I believe is offered by each wine described. The range is 1 to 12, and the great majority of wines mentioned are scored between 8 and 11. This is because most of the wines mentioned are recommended. None this year wins the perfect score of 12, but there are a good number reaching 10 and 11, and these can be regarded as the wines I believe to be the outstanding bargains.

Most wines are scored 8 and 9, which means they come recommended but to me represent good rather than remarkable value. I have been sorely tempted to include some of the really awful wines tasted, which would score 6 or less, but have generally resisted in the interest of trying to maintain reasonable relations with the wine trade! Those few wines marked 7 or less can't be recommended as value for money, but are included for interest.

Wines I have not liked, I have (on the whole) left out. I must admit that these omissions include some of the best-known brands – especially from the United States, from where I have found certain famous names of very disappointing quality.

Also excluded from this edition are sparkling wines. I have found only a very few of the limited number of fizzes available at under £5 at all inspiring. However, because sparklers are very often the subject of special offers in supermarkets, it is possible to pick up useful reductions on fizzes such as own-label cava normally priced at £6–£7 at much nearer the £5 mark. Sainsbury's and Tesco's own-brands are good buys.

Wine boxes are omitted, too. I don't feel they represent any improvement in value for money over bottled wines – and the saving, litre for litre, is rarely more than marginal between box and bottle. And of course there is no such thing as a wine box at under a fiver.

But the principal exclusions in this book are the hundreds of wines I have left out simply because I can't imagine anyone wanting to drink them. Sadly, most of the wines I have tried at under £3.50 or so have been too grim to recommend at any price. But it's overpriced wines that are the prime offenders. There are plenty at £4-plus that wouldn't be good value even at two quid less. And there have been many wines that fail to pass the 'so-what' test. You know, as in answering the question: 'So what do you like about this wine?'. If I have not been able to write down what that is, I cannot recommend the wine. I have to like a wine for a reason, and I have to be able to articulate that reason. Otherwise, I would be in no position to write a book such as this.

I do hope you will enjoy reading and using *Best Wine Buys*. I must, of course, apologise in advance for the inevitable fact that some of the wines mentioned will have been discontinued or displaced with a new vintage or increased in price by the time you are reading this. And I had better show contrition, too, for any disagreements readers may have with me over the comments I have made about individual wines.

Taste is personal in all things, and more so than most when it comes to wine. But I hope the impressions I have given of the hundreds of wines recommended in this guide will tempt to you to try some new flavours, and perhaps even to trade up to a few of the small selections I have made of wines above the £5 limit.

If *Best Wine Buys* arouses your curiosity about the wider world of wine, and encourages you to experiment, then it will have achieved its objective.

The choice

This book categorises the wines by nation of origin. This is largely because retailers sort their wines this way, but also because it is the country or region of origin that still most distinguishes one style of wine from another. True, most wine is now labelled most prominently with its constituent grape variety, but to classify all the world's wines into the small number of principal grape varieties would make for categories of unwieldy size.

Chardonnay and Sauvignon Blanc are overwhelmingly dominant among whites, and four grapes, Cabernet Sauvignon, Merlot, Shiraz and Tempranillo, account for a very high proportion of red wines made worldwide.

But each area of production still – in spite of creeping 'globalisation' – puts its own mark on its wines. Chardonnays from France remain (for the moment at least) quite distinct from those of Australia. Cabernet Sauvignon grown in a cool climate such as that of Bordeaux is a very different wine from Cabernet cultivated in the cauldron of the Barossa.

Of course there are 'styles' that winemakers worldwide seek to follow. Yellow, oaky Chardonnays of the type pioneered in South Australia are now made in South Africa, too – and in new, hi-tech wineries in New Zealand and Chile, Spain and Italy. But the variety is still wide. Even though the 'upfront' high-alcohol wines of the New World have grabbed so much of the market, France continues to make the elegant wines it has always made in its classic regions, Germany still produces racy, delicate Rieslings, and the distinctive zones of Italy, Portugal and Spain make ever more characterful wines from indigenous grapes (as opposed to imported global varieties).

Among less expensive wines, the theme is, admittedly, very much a varietal one. The main selling point for most wines costing under £5 is the grape of origin rather than the country of origin. It makes sense, because the characteristics of various grape varieties do a great deal to identify taste. A bottle of white wine labelled Chardonnay can reasonably be counted on to deliver that distinctive peachy or pineappley smell and soft, unctuous apple flavours. A Sauvignon Blanc should evoke gooseberries, green fruit and crisp freshness. And so on.

As to the best sources of wines under a fiver, it will take only a brief look through this book to reveal that some parts of the world appear to offer a far bigger choice of cheaper wines than others do. The classic regions of France –

Alsace, Bordeaux and Burgundy – make few appearances, simply because their wines are now almost exclusively priced above the £5 threshold – even those of the poorest quality.

The *vins de pays* ('country wines') of France's less-vaunted regions, on the other hand, appear very regularly. So do the wines of southern Italy, the emerging reactivated regions of Portugal and Spain and fast-expanding Argentina. All are proving a growing source of excellent value at under a fiver.

And for all the domination of Chardonnay and Cabernet, there are plenty more grape varieties making their presence felt. Argentina, for example, has revived the fortunes of several French and Italian varieties that had become near-extinct at home. And the grape that (in my view) can make the most exciting of white wines, the Riesling, is now doing great things in the southern hemisphere as well as at home in Germany.

The global varieties are, indeed, everywhere, but this book describes wines made from no fewer than 60 different grape varieties (see the glossary starting on page 128), grown in every corner of the winemaking world. Let's hope this generous and growing choice is the shape of things to come.

A note about vintages

The vintages I have tasted for this new edition should, on the whole, be the ones you'll find on the shelves for most of the life of this book. But inevitably, some 1997 and 1998 wines from the northern hemisphere will be updated from the succeeding vintages. From south of the Equator, some white wines from the 2000 harvest were already making first appearances by late summer of the year, and I have included some of these in this edition.

In France, the general wisdom is that 1998 was a pretty good vintage all round – and on the whole better than 1999. Vin de pays from the southern regions are especially worth looking out for with the 1998 date.

But cheaper wines vary less in quality according to the harvest than grander ones, and when choosing from most of Europe's producing nations, don't worry too much about the year. Don't ignore the maxim, however, that inexpensive dry whites tend to be fresher and more enjoyable the younger they are.

The 2000 harvests in Argentina and Chile have run into some local difficulties, mostly connected to unseasonal rainfall. The word is that 1999 wines are generally of better quality. No such worries in Australia, where quality from one vintage to the next appears to achieve a constancy that must be the envy of all other parts of the winemaking world.

The state of the market

In Britain we drink about a billion bottles of wine each year. It sounds a lot, but comes only to about half a bottle of wine per adult per week. Still, it's a start. Back in 1900, per capita wine consumption here was less than two bottles *per year*. This dismal level continued until the second half of the century, showing improvement only when foreign holidays became the norm, and large numbers of us suddenly discovered a taste for continental vices.

But long before the package-holiday era, Britain was nevertheless an important international market for wine. For centuries, keen imbibers here have been drinking more champagne, claret, Moselle and port than in any other country. So when cheaper wines started to flood in during the 1960s, our wine trade was already geared up to take advantage of the new boom in low-margin plonk.

Unfortunately for the long-established specialist merchants, the supermarkets have scooped most of the market, but Britain has continued to be, as it has always been, the best country in the world in which to buy wine. Not the cheapest, thanks to a long Puritan tradition of trying to repress alcohol consumption through usurious excise duties, but with by far the widest range of sources.

In spite of the high costs prevailing here, Britain drinks more good-quality imported wine than any other country in the world. We are the most valued export market for several of the leading wine-producing nations.

Thus the astounding choice in the shops. Supermarkets carry from 500 to 700 distinct brands. The wine department in Safeway or Tesco can be depended upon to take up more space than bread, or meat. But shopping for wine is a rather more taxing task than choosing a loaf or picking out something for the Sunday roast.

Supermarkets on top

In a nation with so many traditional wine merchants, from grand London purveyors with royal warrants to tiny specialist firms importing the wines of just one region of France, it comes as a shock to find that three-quarters of all the wine bought 'off licence' (for drinking at home) in Britain comes from supermarkets.

But are supermarkets selling quantity at the expense of quality? Not a bit of it. These huge companies take quality very seriously – under £5 (accounting for nine out of every ten bottles sold) as much as over.

Tasting hundreds of supermarket wines every year as I do, I can honestly report finding few I could fairly describe as badly made or unpleasant to drink. But even making allowances for the jading effects of tasting scores of wines at one session, I must confess to one slightly troubling discovery. It is the striking homogeneity of an awful lot of wines. Far too many taste the same as each other.

Fair's fair, there is in some cases a simple explanation for this – because many supermarket 'own-brand' wines *are* the same as each other. Big producers in every part of the world happily apportion their harvests between two, three or more British supermarket chains, bottling the new wine in one giant operation with pauses merely for changing the labels.

And why not? The more outlets there are for the excellent wines of Argentina or Australia, the better. But the sameness problem isn't really about the enviable success of New World exporters. It's more about the uniformity of style. Supermarkets have convinced themselves that they know what their customers want. Most of the wines on the shelves conform not just to the prices dictated by the wine buyers, but to the styles they expect. Safeway, Sainsbury and Tesco all have a hand in making many of the wines they sell, demanding that the products of wineries in every part of the world stick to the styles customers are perceived to demand.

This can hardly be faulted. But wine shoppers who do experiment with different wines on a regular basis will find that there can be a depressing similarity in, say, Chardonnay from sources as diverse as Hungary, Chile, South Africa and the far south of France. The wine-taster's party trick of identifying the nationality of an everyday wine is getting to be a very difficult one to perform with any hope of success.

That said, there is little room for complaint about the supermarkets. There is a terrific choice, and certainly plenty of commendable wines under a fiver. Thus the very extensive sections devoted to some of the supermarkets in the following pages.

High-street combinations

When Britain's two biggest high-street off-licence chains, Thresher and Victoria Wine, announced their 1999 amalgamation under the strikingly odd name 'First

Quench', they proclaimed that their combined network of shops would give them a 15 per cent share of the take-home wine market. It sounds impressive enough until you consider that Tesco alone, through its 566 supermarkets, was already selling more wine than all 3,000 First Quench shops put together.

It puts the traditional off-licence shop firmly in perspective. Had the boom in wine-drinking over the last 20 years not taken place, it seems unlikely even big chains like Threshers would have survived at all in the face of supermarket competition. Whether the strategy of merging into huge nationwide chains will pay off remains to be seen. First Quench has not been having an easy time of it. Whitbread, one of its two brewery co-owners, sold out its half after a very short time, and the whole giant chain is said to be up for sale owing to less-than-exciting profitability.

Off-licences, it might be said, simply aren't cool any more. Wine in particular has become just another grocery item, and specialist retailers in this sector look destined to go the same way as their counterparts in bakery, butchery and fishmongery – by becoming just another aisle or counter in a gigantic hypermarket.

But it's only fair to point out that off-licences are in many ways much more attractive places in which to shop for wine than supermarkets. Prices are quite definitely competitive (it is a myth that supermarket wines are cheap) and if you're prepared to buy a dozen bottles of wine at a time, the likes of Oddbins, Thresher-Victoria Wine, Unwins and Wine Cellars will always give you 10 per cent off – double what can be expected in any supermarket.

Off-licences are forever running special promotions on their wines, too. In the struggle to compete with supermarkets, they have 'loyalty' schemes which outdo store 'points' cards by a mile for value. If you are even an occasional customer at a local branch of a major off-licence chain, don't hesitate to ask about any club-style arrangements they may have.

Fine wine merchants

If the nationwide high-street off-licence chains have been squeezed by the hypermarkets, how much more so for the independently owned specialist wine merchants? It's a testimony to the enterprise of centuries-old firms such as Berry Bros & Rudd in London that they can continue to prosper in the age of the retail multiple – but they do.

Grand old wine merchants can be daunting. It is quite understandable that those proudly proclaiming themselves 'purveyors of fine wines to the Royal

Household' and the like should deter all but the boldest enthusiast in search of something a bit more interesting than this month's special offer at the supermarket.

And it's true that some firms specialising in classed-growth claret and burgundy don't tend to offer much in the way of wines under £5. But this is not a universal truth. Independent merchants are much better placed to offer wines from smaller producers. As can be imagined, most of the world's best wines are made by individual farmer-winemakers rather than by industrial-scale corporations. But supermarkets and shop-chains with hundreds of outlets to stock are not interested in wines made in small quantities. So if you have an adventurous taste for individualistic wines, look to the independent firms, who make a specialism of seeking out interesting small producers.

All the larger independent firms publish a detailed list at least once a year, providing helpful descriptions of all their wines, together with prices, delivery details and so on. If you get on to their mailing lists, they will send you occasional special offers, news of events such as tastings and the occasional 'bin-end' sale. It's all a bit like joining a club – though many temptations to try better and better wines will be put in your way.

The price of wine

How do retailers price their wines? Some bottles seem inexplicably cheap, others unjustifiably expensive. But there is often a simple explanation. Big retailers work to price points. In wine, these are £2.99, £3.49, £3.99 and so on. You'll find very few bottles priced anywhere between these 50p spacings. A wine that wouldn't be profitable at £2.99 but would be at, say, £3.11 is priced at £3.49 in the hope that shoppers won't be wise to the fact that it is relatively poor value.

It's true that there are some wines on supermarket shelves priced at £3.29, £3.79 etc. But these price points occur with suspicious irregularity, and suggest that an awful lot of wines are being pushed the greater distance towards the next 49p and 99p points.

Price can be a poor guide to quality even at the best of times. The only means by which any of us can determine a wine's value is personal taste. The ideal bottle is one you like very much and would buy again at the same price without demur.

But just for curiosity's sake, it's fun to know what the wine itself actually costs, and what the retailer is making on it. So let's look at how the costs break down in a French wine costing £4.49 at a mythical supermarket we'll call Safeco. This is a slightly unusual purchase by a supermarket, because the wine is being bought direct from the vineyard where it was made. Usually, retail multiples buy their wines by a less strenuous method, from agents and distributors in the UK.

Price paid by Safeco to supplier in France for the bottled wine	£1.40
Transport and insurance to UK	£0.28
Excise duty	£1.16
Cost to Safeco	£2.84
Safeco's routine mark-up at 30%	£0.85
VAT at 17.5% on marked-up price	£0.65
Provisional shelf price	£4.34
Adjustment in price/VAT to price point	£0.15
Shelf price in Safeco	£4.49

The largest share of the money appears to go to the producer in France. But from his £1.40 he must pay the cost of growing and harvesting the grapes, pressing them, fermenting the juice, clarifying and treating the wine. Then he must bottle, cork, encapsulate, label and pack the wine into cartons. If his margin after these direct costs is 50p, he's doing well.

The prime profiteer, however, is not the supermarket, even though it makes a healthy £1 in mark-up. It is the Chancellor who does best, by miles. Excise duty and VAT are two of the cheapest taxes to collect – less than 1 per cent of revenue raised – and from this single bottle of wine, the Treasury trousers a princely £1.84.

Travellers to wine-producing countries are always thrilled to find that by taking their own bottles, jugs or giant demi-johns to rustic vineyards offering wine from the cask they can buy drinkable stuff for as little as 50p a litre. What too few travellers appreciate is that, for the wine itself, that's about what the supermarkets are paying for it. When enjoying your sub-£5 bottle of wine, it is interesting to reflect on the economic reality known as 'added value' – which dictates that the worthiest person in the chain, the producer, has probably earned less than 10 per cent of the final price.

Wine on the web

The new millennium dawned amidst a fever of enthusiasm for e-commerce. One household in five, we were told, is equipped to use the internet, and in no time half of us will be shopping online, just as they do in the USA. The demise of some big dotcom names and the collapse of hi-tech share values have done something to dampen this early enthusiasm, but the trend is still clear.

Wine seems an obvious candidate for this method of retailing, and a raft of new enterprises has sprung up to exploit the emerging market. Names include carousewine, chateauonline, everywine, itswine, madaboutwine. The indelicately named orgasmicwine has been subsumed into Virgin Wines, the biggest of the new 'e-tailers' launched by Sir Richard Branson in summer 2000 with the pledge that virginwine.com would have annual sales of £100 million within the next five years.

Can this sort of promise really bear fruit? A big, well-capitalised business like Virgin might have a chance, with its list of 500 wines and its claim to have ready access to 20,000 others – and all offered, says Branson, at the lowest prices anywhere. But few other wine.com traders are in a position to sell themselves on such a basis. Smaller companies don't like to hold wine in stock. They would have to pay the supplier for it, hand over the duty and VAT to Customs, and finance the storage. The upshot is that merchants trading exclusively on the web tend to be 'virtual' rather than actual wine merchants. Only when they receive a customer's order will they request the goods from their supplier and pay the requisite duty and tax. Not much chance, then, of next-day delivery for the customer – which rather undermines the claimed immediacy of e-commerce.

Choice is another issue. Most e-tailers have very short lists of wine, bulked out by mixed-case offers or 'bin-end sales'. It seems that it is not yet practical to display, price and annotate more than a few dozen wines on a website. But for high-street merchants and supermarkets it's another story. The chains have head-office lists of as many as 700 different wines, but can't hope to offer the whole lot in any but their very biggest outlets. On the web, however, it's no problem. A favourite wine you can find in a Tesco superstore but not in a dinky Tesco 'Metro' branch will be guaranteed to be found on the Tesco website (if and when Tesco manage to create a genuinely comprehensive and accessible site, that is). The price will be the same as it is in the shop, and delivery will be dependable – and free for orders worth a reasonable minimum.

How can the new e-tailers possibly compete? They have no shop window other than the web. It is not possible to buy a single bottle of wine to taste before deciding whether to go for a case or two. How can a web-only trader provide 'customer service'? A duff bottle bought from a supermarket (on the web or not) can be returned to any branch for a replacement and/or refund (yes, some supermarkets give both), but how do you return bad wine to cyberspace? There will always be lingering doubts about reliability. Will wines have been stored correctly? Will delivery be guaranteed? Will credit card payment to an unfamiliar e-tailer be secure?

At this stage, I cannot safely recommend shopping anywhere on the web for wine other than from the sites of well-established retailers, whether supermarkets, high-street operators like Majestic and Oddbins, or specialised independent merchants. For these retailers, of course, internet trading is little more than an extension of their existing home-delivery operations. The only difference is that their lists can be viewed on screen instead of on paper, and orders can be placed by the same credit card over the net rather than over the phone, by fax or (perish the thought) in an envelope with a stamp on it.

The 'traditional' retailers, if names like Oddbins and Tesco can really be described as such, are going to prove tough (I believe unbeatable) competition for the new online traders. The dotcom firms have spent a fortune recruiting people from the traditional trade – and the press – to give a professional gloss to their sites, but there is nothing they can do to improve on the quality, diversity or price of wine already on offer.

But these are very early days for internet shopping. The wine trade is predicting a shake-out of the dozens of new e-merchants during the next year or so as market share is, or is not, established. In the meantime, web-shoppers will be well advised to order wine only from enterprises that inspire confidence.

Cross-Channel shopping

Choosing wine at French prices is a lot more fun than surfing the web, but is it really worth travelling across the Channel for the sole purpose of stocking up for a few pounds less than you would pay at home? The short answer is yes. It's fun to visit France (or even, at a pinch, Belgium) and out of season it can be very cheap. High-speed ferries, catamarans and hovercraft can carry you to historic Channel ports in an hour or two for just a few pounds if you take advantage of the perpetual ticket promotions run in the national press. Discounted tickets through the Eurotunnel are never quite as cheap, but for train enthusiasts, the journey is a treat in itself.

True, there is no longer any duty-free shopping on board the ferries (there never was on the trains). But as passengers on P&O Stena, SeaFrance and Hoverspeed have been discovering since the abolition of the old tax perk in 1999, this has made no difference. You can still buy wine, spirits and other goodies on board the ships at prices that seem remarkably adjacent to those pertaining in the good old days of duty-free.

The reason for this curious continuity is that shipping companies are now buying their supplies duty-paid on the other side of the Channel – which in some cases is almost as cheap as buying those supplies on a duty-free basis used to be. After all, the duty on wine in France is only 2p a 75cl bottle. In Spain, Italy and elsewhere in southern Europe, there's no duty on wine at all. VAT in France, at 20.6 per cent, is appreciably higher than the prevailing rate of 17.5 per cent here, but ferry operators are absorbing the cost.

In effect, the ships are in direct competition with the supermarkets and hideous British-owned 'wine warehouses' in the Channel ports. But ferry operators cannot hope, really, to compete with France's huge and powerful hypermarket companies. Auchan, Cora, Continent, LeClerc and other retail multiples have enormous buying power and of course very much larger premises in which to display their goods. And the car park of a major out-of-town *hypermarché* has rather more room in which to manoeuvre a groaning trolley than does the vehicle deck of a roll-on-roll-off ferry.

As explained in the feature on page 19, wine prices are dramatically lower in French supermarkets than they are in their British counterparts. But there is a dramatic gap, too, between prices in British supermarkets either side of the water. You can discover this by visiting Tesco's 'Vin Plus' branch in the immense

Cité Europe shopping centre at the Pas de Calais (near the Eurotunnel terminal) or Sainsbury's newly enlarged drinks shop next to the mega Auchan supermarket in Calais.

I am much obliged to Sainsbury's for sending me a list of their wine prices on both sides of the Channel. The difference is so spectacular that I cannot resist reproducing a few of the highlights. Remember, the difference in excise duty between the two countries is £1.14 per bottle (£1.16 in UK, 2p in France), but French VAT is higher, at 20.6p per £1-worth of wine, compared to 17.5p per £1-worth in Britain. So, if duty and VAT were the only differentials, a bottle of wine valued at £2 including mark-up by a French retailer would sell for £2.44, and for £3.71 in a British shop – a price difference of about 50 per cent. But as Sainsbury's own figures dramatically demonstrate, the differential is actually far greater.

Wine	UK	France	Price difference
Sainsbury's Bordeaux Blanc	£3.29	£1.45	127%
Sainsbury's Claret	£3.99	£1.75	128%
Muscadet	£2.79	£1.25	124%
Sainsbury's Anjou Blanc	£2.99	£1.25	139%
Sainsbury's Liebfraumilch	£2.89	£1.10	162%
Sainsbury's Mosel 1.5cl	£5.95	£2.10	185%
Sainsbury's Sicilia Red	£2.99	£1.05	185%
Viña Albali Reserva	£4.49	£2.25	100%
Sainsbury's Aus Chardonnay	£3.99	£1.95	105%
Sainsbury's Mendoza Red	£3.29	£1.25	163%

These differences are astonishing – and far in excess of anything accounted for by mere differences in tax. But Sainsbury's is still nothing like as cheap as some of the local retailers in Channel ports, where very drinkable *vin de pays* can start at as little as 6FF, or 60p at around the current exchange rate.

And the fact is that it is infinitely more exciting to shop in the French *hypermarchés* than it ever can be to take the cautious route into just another Sainsbury or Tesco. Just about everything in French supermarkets is cheaper – not just the wine, spirits and beers – and there is a choice of fresh and preserved foods in the larger superstores that puts our own supermarkets to shame. English is widely spoken, and bilingual signs are commonplace in the stores. And if you're using an appropriate credit card, paying the bill is no more complicated than it is in a supermarket at home.

There is no limit to the quantity or value of goods you can bring back from any EU member country, provided it is not intended for resale in the UK. British Customs and Excise long ago published 'guidelines' as to what they consider are reasonable limits on drinks that can be deemed to be for 'personal consumption'. You can thus import, no questions asked, 90 litres of wine, 20 of fortified wine, 10 of spirits and 110 of beer. That's about as much as a couple travelling together (and therefore able to import twice the above quantities) could cram into a family car without threatening the well-being of its suspension.

Savings on beer and spirits are, if anything, even more dramatic than they are on wine. French duty on beer is 5p a pint, compared to 33p here. This means a case of beer typically costing £12–£15 here can be had for under a fiver in Calais. It seems crazy. Similarly, a 70cl bottle of London gin or Scotch whisky costing £11–£12 here is yours for £7–£8 in France, where duty on spirits is half the £5.48 charged here and mark-ups lower.

As if these differentials were not enough, the Channel ports also teem with good-value restaurants and hotels. Boulogne and Calais, Dieppe and Dunkirk bristle with venues where you can enjoy a 100-franc menu of a standard that would set you back several times as much back home. And there are respectable hotels where a clean room with bath or shower en suite, plus croissants and excellent coffee for breakfast, can be had for £25 all in.

Why are wines so much cheaper in French shops?

The price gaps between the big stores either side of the Channel are, as illustrated above, by no means entirely accounted for by the difference between UK excise duty and VAT and French duty and VAT. So what's going on?

It's not that British supermarkets charge higher margins than their continental counterparts. True, the Office of Fair Trading's Competition Commissioner is currently investigating allegations that supermarkets are overcharging customers. But when it comes to wine, the differential between the same wine on sale in the Asda at Coventry and the Auchan at Calais arises from how those respective supermarkets apply their margins.

It goes like this. In France, retailers typically mark up wines at 30 per cent. In the UK, as it happens, retailers also mark up by around 30 per cent. The difference is that shops in Britain add the mark-up not to the basic value of the wine, but to the duty-paid and delivered (DPD) price.

In the UK, every bottle of still wine, regardless of quality or price, comes with an excise duty and shipping cost of around £1.40. So a bottle of wine the retailer buys for £1 from the producer has a DPD price of £2.40. Marked up by 30 per cent for the retailer's margin, that becomes £3.12. Add VAT at 17.5 per cent and the actual retail price turns into £3.66.

In France, it's very different. The typical duty and shipping cost in the price of a bottle of French wine is 12p. So the DPD price of the £1 bottle is £1.12. Marked up by 30 per cent it becomes £1.32. Add French VAT at 20.6 per cent and the actual retail price is £1.59. That's more than £2 less than the price of the same bottle of wine on our side of the Channel.

The difference is inflated because British retailers charge their 30 per cent on the DPD price rather than on what they've paid to the producer. As well as paying the extra shipping cost plus the £1.10 differential between UK excise duty (£1.16) and French (2p) you're paying a further 38p of retailer mark-up here.

The best buys

'Which is your favourite wine?' is a familiar question to anyone who writes on this subject. It's impossible to answer without several qualifications – red or white, sweet or dry, under £5 or over £5. But in the context of this book, it's relatively straightforward. Here are the wines that, this year, I have rated most highly for value by giving them scores of 10 (first division) or 11 (premier league) out of the maximum 12. All are, I believe, top value for money. They are not placed in any order other than alphabetically and in ascending price.

Premier league

Reds

Karalta Shiraz Cabernet 1999	£3.49	*Asda*
Viña Armantes Garnacha 1999	£3.99	*Majestic*
Viña Fuerte Garnacha, Calatayud, 1999	£3.99	*Waitrose*
Sainsbury's South African Cabernet Sauvignon	£4.29	*Sainsbury*

Whites

Riesling QbA, Friedrich-Wilhelm Gymnasium, 1991	£3.99	*Majestic*
Avelsbacher Hammerstein Riesling QbA, Trier State Domain, 1992	£4.49	*Majestic*
Miranda White Pointer 1999	£4.49	*Tesco*
Pinot Blanc, Cave de Turckheim, 1999	£4.49	*Booths, First Quench, Unwins*
Alsace Gewürztraminer, Cave de Turckheim, 1998	£4.99	*Booths*
Canepa Winemaker's Selection Gewürztraminer 1999	£4.99	*Sainsbury*
Lindemans Bin 65 Chardonnay 1999	£4.99	*Booths, Co-op, First Quench, Majestic, Oddbins, Safeway, Sainsbury, Somerfield, Tesco, Unwins*

Amazingly cheap for the quality – a soft and spicy blend with a finely edged finish.

First division

Reds

Safeway Sicilian Red 1999	£2.99	*Safeway*
Sainsbury's Sicilia Red	£2.99	*Sainsbury*
Sainsbury's Syrah Vin de Pays d'Oc 1998	£2.99	*Sainsbury*
Somerfield Côtes du Roussillon, Jean Jean, 1998	£2.99	*Somerfield*
Somerfield Sicilian Red 1998	£2.99	*Somerfield*
Somerfield Syrah Vin de Pays d'Oc, Jean Jean	£2.99	*Somerfield*
Ramada 1999	£3.49	*First Quench, Safeway, Sainsbury*
Safeway Syrah Vin de Pays d'Oc 1998	£3.49	*Safeway*
Somerfield Minervois 1998	£3.49	*Somerfield*
Picajuan Peak Sangiovese 1998	£3.79	*Tesco*
Adiseño Tempranillo 1999	£3.99	*Co-op*
Carta Vieja Merlot 1999	£3.99	*Safeway*
Corazon Bonarda 1999	£3.99	*First Quench*
Domaine de Petit Roubié Syrah 1999	£3.99	*Booths*
Firriato Nero d'Avola Syrah 1998	£3.99	*Somerfield, Waitrose*
Il Padrino 1999	£3.99	*Oddbins*
Minervois, Domaine Roche Vue, 1998	£3.99	*Safeway*
Palmela 1998	£3.99	*Safeway*
Penta Cabernet Sauvignon-Malbec 1999	£3.99	*Unwins*
Picajuan Peak Malbec 1998	£3.99	*Tesco*
Portada 1997	£3.99	*Somerfield, Unwins, Wine Cellar*
Rio de Plata Cabernet Sauvignon 1996	£3.99	*Co-op, Londis*
Safeway Argentinian Bonarda 1999	£3.99	*Safeway*
Safeway Oak Aged Côtes du Rhône 1999	£3.99	*Safeway*
Somerfield Argentine Sangiovese 1999	£3.99	*Somerfield*
Tesco Chilean Malbec 1999	£3.99	*Tesco*
Saumur Rouge Les Nivières 1998	£4.25	*Waitrose*
Bright Brothers Vistalba Malbec 1999	£4.29	*Sainsbury*
Castillo de Almansa Reserva 1994	£4.49	*Booths*
Domaine du Moulin The Cabernets 1998	£4.49	*Waitrose*
Espiral Tempranillo Cabernet Sauvignon 1998	£4.49	*Unwins*
Primitivo Merum 1998	£4.49	*Unwins, Waitrose*
Segada Trincadeira Preta-Castelao 1999	£4.49	*Sainsbury, Unwins*
Palmeras Estate Cabernet Sauvignon 1996	£4.89 *Booths*,	£4.99 *Safeway*

Beyers Truter Pinotage 1998	£4.99	Tesco
Carmesi 1998	£4.99	Tesco
Chapel Hill Barrique Aged Cabernet Sauvignon 1997	£4.99	Safeway, Tesco
Château Pech-Latt 1998	£4.99	Waitrose
Côtes du Ventoux, Vidal Fleury, 1998	£4.99	Majestic
Dama de Toro, Bodegas Farina, 1998	£4.99	Sainsbury
Dão Dom Ferraz 1997	£4.99	Booths, First Quench, Tesco
Los Robles Carmenère 1999	£4.99	Sainsbury
Lindemans Bin 50 Shiraz 1999	£4.99	Asda, Co-op, Londis, Majestic, Oddbins, Sainsbury, Tesco, Unwins, Wine Cellar
Norton Barbera 1997	£4.99	Wine Cellar
Norton Malbec 1997	£4.99	Tesco, Unwins, Wine Cellar
Pendulum Zinfandel 1999	£4.99	Waitrose
Prosperity Red	£4.99	Majestic
Santa Ines Carmenere 1998	£4.99	Tesco
Santa Julia Oak Aged Tempranillo 1999	£4.99	Sainsbury
Serrano Rosso Conero 1999	£4.99	Sainsbury
Undurraga Pinot Noir 1999	£4.99	Tesco
Viña del Recuerdo 1997	£4.99	First Quench
Viña Porta Reserve Cabernet Sauvignon 1998	£4.99	Unwins
Woolpunda Shiraz 1998	£4.99	Tesco

Whites

Cuvée Philippe Gers 1999	£2.49	Unwins
Broken Bridge Chardonnay Colombard 1999	£2.99	Waitrose
Sainsbury's Sicilia White	£2.99	Sainsbury
Somerfield Sicilian White 1998	£2.99	Somerfield
Woodcutter's White 1999	£2.99	Safeway
Mirrabook Chardonnay 1999	£3.29	Majestic
Domaine Le Puts Blanc, Michel Bordes, 1999	£3.39	Majestic
Asda Argentinian Torrontes 2000	£3.49	Asda
Canepa Semillon 1999	£3.99	Unwins
Clos de Monestier, Bergerac Sec, 1999	£3.99	Booths
Culemborg Unwooded Chardonnay 1999	£3.99	Waitrose
Les Fontanelles Viognier Foncalieu 1999	£3.99	Majestic
Graacher Himmelreich Riesling Spätlese 1997	£3.99	Co-op
Kendermanns Dry Riesling 1998	£3.99	Co-op, First Quench, Oddbins, Sainsbury, Tesco, Waitrose

La Cité Chardonnay 1999	£3.99	Waitrose
Lindemans Cawarra Semillon Chardonnay 1999	£3.99	Booths, Co-op, First Quench, Londis, Majestic, Oddbins, Sainsbury
Les Marionettes Marsanne 1997	£3.99	Somerfield
Orvieto Classico Abboccato 1999	£3.99	Tesco
Santa Catalina Verdejo Sauvignon 1998	£3.99	Somerfield
Sartori Organic Soave 1999	£3.99	Sainsbury
Tesco Mexican Chardonnay 1999	£3.99	Tesco
Vin de Pays Côtes de Gascogne, Vivian Ducourneau, 1999	£3.99	Majestic
Lindemans Cawarra Chardonnay 1999	£4.49	Asda, Booths, Co-op, First Quench, Londis, Majestic, Safeway, Sainsbury, Wine Cellar
Lustau Moscatel de Chipiona	£4.49	Waitrose
Picajuan Peak Viognier 1999	£4.49	Tesco
Trulli Chardonnay 1999	£4.99	Co-op, Oddbins, Somerfield
Pinot Blanc D'Alsace, Blanck, 1998	£4.95	Waitrose
Bernkasteler Badstube Riesling Kabinett, Jacobus, 1994	£4.99	Majestic
Cono Sur Gewürztraminer 1999	£4.99	Asda, Tesco
Cranswick Estate Marsanne 1998	£4.99	Asda
Cuckoo Hill Chardonnay Viognier 1998	£4.99	Waitrose
Domaine de L'Olivette 1999	£4.99	Waitrose
L'Enclos Domeque Marsanne-Roussanne 1999	£4.99	Waitrose
Inycon Chardonnay 1999	£4.99	Sainsbury
Marsanne/Roussanne en Barrique 1999	£4.99	Unwins
Muscat de Beaumes de Venise	£4.99	Waitrose
Prosperity White	£4.99	Majestic
Samos Vin Doux Naturel	£4.99	Unwins
Soave Classico Monte Tenda, Tedeschi, 1998	£4.99	Majestic
Vouvray La Couronne des Plantagenets 1999	£4.99	Sainsbury
Wehlener Sonnenuhr Riesling Kabinett, Jacobus, 1992	£4.99	Majestic
Wynns Coonawarra Riesling 1999	£4.99	Booths, Majestic, Oddbins, Sainsbury, Wine Cellar
Yalumba Viognier 1997	£4.99	Tesco

The retailers

In this edition, I have focused attention on the largest retailers around the country, giving more space this year to the major supermarket chains. They do, after all, account for three-quarters of all take-home wine sales.

The 'big five' of Asda, Safeway, Sainsbury, Somerfield and Tesco are here in depth. So is Waitrose, which, in spite of confining its shops so strictly on a geographical basis (namely England's high-earning southern regions), has easily the widest and most exciting range of any of the supermarkets – and offers the entire list to mail-order customers nationwide.

The excellent north-west England supermarket chain EH Booth is here, but that other northern chain, Morrisons, is not. This latter omission is occasioned not by preference, but because for some reason I cannot persuade Morrisons' wine department to communicate with me. It is not possible to include any assessment of a retailer's wines (even if I go out and buy them all) without their co-operation.

One other notable exclusion is Marks & Spencer. As in the previous year, I bought a number of wines for tasting (having not been honoured with an invitation to the press tasting) but found those wines I did try to be almost universally uninspiring – to my taste, at any rate. Having not had a chance to taste a wider range, I have not been able to compile an entry of a size that would be useful.

As to the high-street off-licences, I was sad that the chain of likeable wine shops operated by the famous London brewery Fuller's threw in the towel and sold out to Unwins. But the good news is that many of the wines familiar to Fuller's followers have now been incorporated into the range of the now very large Unwins chain.

Takeovers in the high street will continue. First Quench (Thresher, Victoria Wine, etc.) is said to be for sale, and Oddbins, now in the ownership of a huge French company, is still the subject of sale rumours.

But there's a lot of wine out there, and still plenty of it under a fiver.

ASDA

Once upon a time, Asda had a seriously interesting range of wines. There were a few boring years, and then along came Wal-Mart. It's too soon to say what the effect of being taken over by the world's biggest retailer will be, and there have been few exciting changes yet to the wine range, but Asda must surely be a supermarket to watch – especially from the price of point of view.

Asda prices are, indeed, interesting. They do undercut other retailers, although by no means universally, and many of their wines avoid those suspicious 'price points' – always ending in a 9 and usually a 99 – that make you wonder by how much the price must have been jacked up to get there.

In common with other supermarkets, Asda varies the choice of wines it offers according to individual branches. It came as a surprise to me to be told that the greatly hyped Asda/Wal-Mart megastore in Bristol, which opened in the summer of 2000, has a mere 170 different wines. A Tesco half that size might typically have a choice nearer 500.

But it's certainly not the breadth of the choice that counts for most. Asda does have a decent range and good prices and – like all other supermarkets – offers regular discounts on a range of wines every month.

Dark ruby colour and raspberry nose on this cherry-fruit red from the Loire valley.

RED WINES

ARGENTINA

£2.99 (10) Asda Argentinian Red — *A consistent bargain for many years, this soft middleweight has a lot more ripeness and balance than might be expected at the very low price*

£4.49 (9) Far Flung Cabernet Sauvignon Merlot 1999 — *Glyceriny, young, purply-black heavyweight (14% alcohol) with nearly overripe spiritousness; good, though, and it will improve over time*

AUSTRALIA

£3.49 (11) Karalta Shiraz Cabernet 1999 — *This is incredibly cheap for a good-quality Australian red; just the right match of soft 'n' spicy upfront fruit and edginess at the finish*

£4.99 (10) Lindemans Bin 50 Shiraz 1999 — *Dark and spicy, super-ripe middleweight (13.5% alcohol) has a delicious toasted-nut heart; a food wine – try game stews*

£4.99 (9) Lindemans Cawarra Shiraz Cabernet 1999 — *Nicely balanced middleweight with a tang of bitterness (hint of gravy browning?) on the finish; a food wine*

CHILE

£4.98 (8) Cono Sur Pinot Noir 1999 — *Valiant attempt to capture the fleshy strawberry style of Burgundy; interesting rather than exciting*

FRANCE

£4.23 (9) Domaine des Hardières, Anjou Villages, 1999 — *Dark ruby colour and summery raspberry nose on this Loire slurper with crisp cherry fruit; a wine with character*

£4.48 (9) Fitou, Château Lahore Bergez, 1997 — *Lean but by no means thin red with spice and clean finish, from a well-known Languedoc AC; benefits from its maturity*

| £4.99 | (9) | James Herrick Cuvée Simone 1998 | *Very decent mass-market vin de pays d'Oc with soft but firm berry fruit; has the warm spiciness of a good-quality Rhône* |

ITALY

| £4.99 | (8) | Pendulum Zinfandel 1999 | *Italian rendering of a California theme, and it's even made by a company called MGM; browny colour, chocolatey, creamy, plummy-raisiny character; interesting* |

WHITE WINES

ARGENTINA

£2.99	(9)	Asda Argentinian White	*'Crisp aromatic' white is in fact rather soft, but certainly aromatic; pleasant tropical fruit and clean finish – and a keen price*
£3.49	(10)	Asda Argentinian Torrontes 2000	*Super grapey-nosed, soft fruit-salad yet dry, fresh white from Argentina's muscat-like, indigenous white grape*
£4.97	(9)	Far Flung Viognier 1999	*Insinuating, weighty, dry wine with richness and an apricot note – and 13.5% alcohol*

AUSTRALIA

£3.97	(10)	Hardys Stamp Series Chardonnay Semillon 1999	*Evergreen Aussie standby; fresh blend of exotic fruit and clean acidity – and 10 per cent cheaper here than elsewhere*
£3.99	(9)	Karalta Semillon 1999	*Good colour and a recognisable banana nose; hints of unction and honey in a fresh wine with perky fruit*
£4.49	(10)	Lindemans Cawarra Chardonnay 1999	*Zesty, minerally, unoaked style to this popular brand; has weight and a creamy hint, balanced by a refreshing lemon acidity; clever stuff*